This book is all about

....

Our Baby

Introduction

Every child is delightfully unique, and so are the joys (and the difficulties) of the early years of parenthood, as everyone blessed with children will know.

There are many events and occasions in the early years which are well worth recording. The days and weeks slip by fast and what seems unforgettable on the day can easily disappear from memory within a month or two. So this book has been prepared to help you record facts and incidents during pregnancy and the first four years of your child's life.

The sequence followed reflects the usual stages of child development. Additional pages have been included for memories of birthdays, Christmas and holidays during the first four years. Medical history is an important topic to record clearly. Several pages have been provided for this, and for developmental tests at different ages. 'Our Baby' will become a source of information as well as recollections.

It may be that one day, when your offspring has become taller than you are and is off making a living in the world – and perhaps has made you a grandparent – the events and impressions you have recorded in this book will refresh your memories of much that is best in these early childhood years.

Contents

Ante-natal Care

Weight gain during the pregnancy	
6 weeks	30 weeks
12 weeks	36 weeks
18 weeks	40 weeks
24 weeks	

Expected date of delivery

Illnesses during pregnancy

Name of consultant

Hospital number

Favourite foods/dislikes

Comments

Ante-natal classes attended

....

....

Teachers

....

Exercise classes attended

....

....

Teachers

....

Swimming classes attended

....

....

Teachers

....

....

Scan Pictures

The Birth

Born on (date) .... at (time) ....

Place ....

Delivered by (midwife) ....

Weight at birth .... Length at birth ....

Head measurement ....

Colour of eyes ....

Colour of hair ....

Other distinguishing features ....

....

Star sign ....

The people who came to visit were
....

....

....

....

....

Photograph

....

....

....

....

....

....

....

Birth Announcements

Gifts and flowers received

	from
	from
	from
	from
	from
	from
	from
	from

This is the way the birth was announced

Congratulations

Some of the cards people sent

Coming Home

We came home on
....

Our address was
....

....

The weather was
....

These were the people there to greet us
....

....

The midwife first visited on
....

....

The health visitor first came on
....

....

Other memories of the first few days

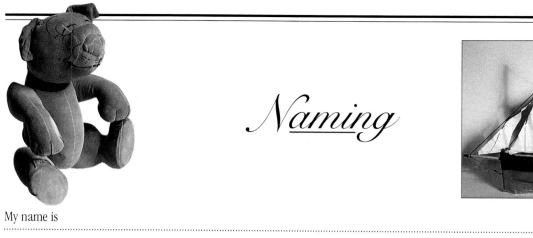

Naming

My name is
....

My parents chose this name because
....

Photograph

My christening or naming day party took place
....

on (date)
....

at (place)
....

I wore
....
....

My godparents were
....
....
....

How the occasion was celebrated
....
....
....
....
....

Presents received

	from
....	from
....	from
....	from
....	from
....	from

Family Tree

Great Grandparents

Great Grandparents

Grandparents

Grandparents

Father

Mother

Brothers

Our Baby

Sisters

Uncles	Aunts	Cousins

First Time

I first began to watch my mother when I was
....

I first smiled on
....

I first laughed on
....

The first time I saw myself in a mirror was on
....

I discovered my hands on
....

I first reached out and took a toy on
....

I first made cooing noises on
....

I discovered my feet on
....

I recognised my name at
....

I learned to point at things when I was
....

Photograph

I first waved goodbye on
....

....

I first copied sounds my parents made on
....

....

....

....

....

My hair was first cut on
....

....

....

....

....

Bedtime

My sleeping pattern at the beginning was

first slept through the night on

The things I liked best at bedtime were (hand stroking, lullabies)

Favourite bedtime stories:

Favourite bedtime toys:

ALL GONE !

Eating

I was breast fed/bottle fed until

I had my first taste of solid food on

The food was

I was eating well from a spoon by

I started eating finger foods on

These foods were

I was fully weaned by

I could drink from a spout cup by

I could feed myself by

Favourite foods:

Foods not liked:

First Moves

I first rolled over on
....

I first sat without support on
....

I first began to move myself around on
....

I did this by means of
....

I first crawled on
....

....

Photograph

Photograph

Walking

could pull myself to my feet by the age of

could walk around holding on to the furniture by the age of

could stand alone by the age of

took my first steps on my own on

first wore shoes on

they were coloured   and their size was

Photograph

Photograph

Favourite Things

(at 3 months)

Favourite toys and games:
....
....
....

Favourite lullabies:
....
....
....

(at 6 months)

Favourite foods:
....
....

Favourite toys and games:
....
....

Favourite songs:
....
....
....

(at 1 year)

Favourite clothes:
....
....

Favourite books:
....
....

Favourite foods:
....
....

Favourite toys and games:
....
....

Favourite songs:
....
....

Favourite videos:
....
....

My best friend was:
....
....
....

Hands and Feet

Tracing of hand at   months, and at   months

(draw round a hand, and again a few months later to see how much it has grown)

Tracing of foot at   months, and at   months

(draw round a foot, and again a few months later to see how much it has grown)

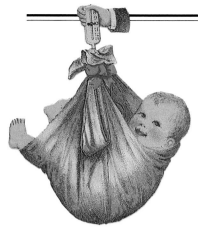

Weighing In

Date	Age	Head Circumference	Length	Weight		
				kg	lbs	oz

Growth Charts

Weight Chart

Weight in
kilograms
(pounds)

—— Boys 50th centile
—— Girls 50th centile

Height Chart

Length in
centimetres
(inches)

—— Boys 50th centile
—— Girls 50th centile

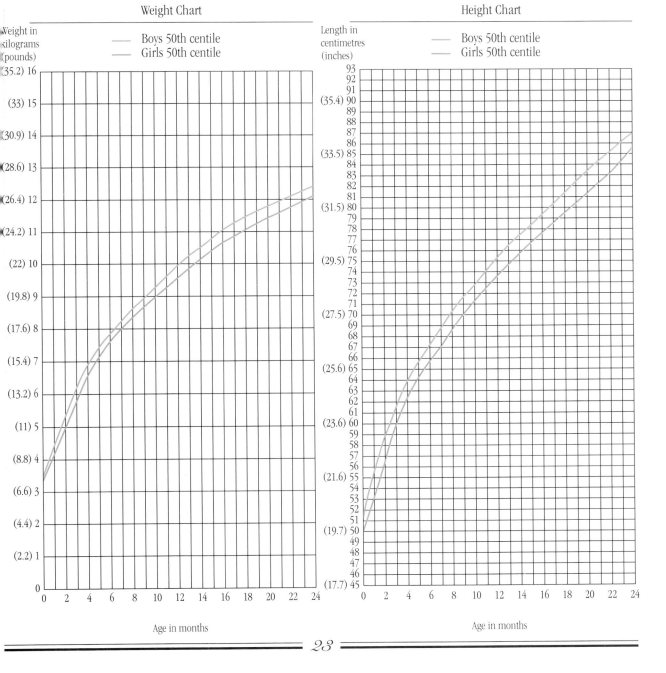

Age in months

Age in months

First Teeth

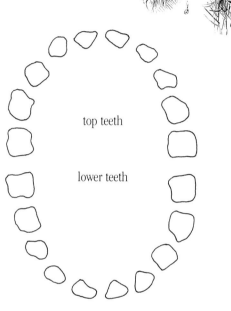

(Write in on the diagram the month each tooth appeared)

1st tooth (date)

2nd tooth (date)

3rd tooth (date)

4th tooth (date)

5th tooth (date)

I had all my first teeth aged

My first visit to the dentist was on

top teeth

lower teeth

Photograph

Photograph

Health

National Health Service number:

....

Blood group:

....

Family doctor's name:

Address:

....

....

Telephone number:

....

Emergency telephone number:

....

Health visitor's name:

Clinic name:

....

Address:

....

....

Telephone number:

....

Clinic times:

....

Dentist's name

Address:

....

....

Telephone number:

....

Medical Record

Immunisation Record	
1st Diphtheria, Whooping cough, Tetanus (DTP)	date given
2nd Diphtheria, Whooping cough, Tetanus (DTP)	date given
3rd Diphtheria, Whooping cough, Tetanus (DTP)	date given
1st Poliomyelitis	date given
2nd Poliomyelitis	date given
3rd Poliomyelitis	date given
1st Hib	date given
2nd Hib	date given
3rd Hib	date given
Measles, Mumps and Rubella (MMR)	date given
BCG	date given
Diphtheria and Tetanus booster	date given
Poliomyelitis booster	date given

Record of Illnesses

Allergies and Drugs

Convalescent FRANK HOLL (1845–1888)
Christopher Wood Gallery, London/Bridgeman Art Library

Development Tests

(Note how your child was tested, by whom and the reactions and results)

6 weeks

1 year

2 years

3 years

Did your child need any additional checks?

Hearing Tests	
Date	Results
Date	Results
Date	Results

Eye Tests	
Date	Results
Date	Results
Date	Results

Comments

ALL GONE!

Early Milestones

started to understand words when I was

could get upstairs by myself at

could go downstairs by myself when I was

y means of

first helped my mummy on

oing

first helped my daddy on

oing

could point to parts of my body when I was

could run when I was

could use a spoon when I was

built a tower with blocks when I was

Early Achievements

(from 14 months)

My first words were

....

....

....

....

What I called things and people		
Name of thing or person	My word for it	Age

I could say or sing a nursery rhyme at

It was

....

....

....

....

could take my clothes off at
....

first threw a ball at
....

first kicked a ball at
....

could recognise and name three colours by
....

could pedal a trike by
....

could draw a circle by
....

could draw a straight line by
....

could draw a face by
....

could draw a person by
....

could dress myself by
....

could use a knife and fork by
....

could write my name by
....

learnt to swim when I was
....

first rode a bike when I was
....

rode a bike without stabilisers when I was
....

Photograph

Photograph

Hospital

My first emergency visit to hospital was on
....

I went there because
....

Attendance and Admissions			
Date	Hospital	Doctor/Consultant	Reason/Treatment

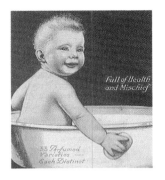

Bathtime

My favourite bathtime toys were

....

....

....

The people who I liked to bath me were

....

....

....

The games I liked to play were

....

....

....

....

Photograph

Potty Training

I first sat on a potty when I was

....

My first dry day was

....

My first day at home without nappies was

....

My first outing without nappies was

....

I started to go to the toilet on my own when I was

....

I was dry at night by

....

Child Care

The mother and toddler groups I went to were
....

....

These are the names of some of the friends I played with
....

....

....

My childminder's or nanny's name was
....

....

My babysitters' names were
....

....

....

The day nursery I went to was
....

....

The people who looked after me were
....

....

....

The playgroup I went to was
....

....

The people who looked after me there were
....

....

....

My friends' names at playgroup were
....

....

....

Nursery School

The nursery school I went to was
....

....

This is how I used to get there
....

....

Teachers' names:
....

....

The pets we had at nursery were
....

....

This is what we did at Christmas
....

....

This is what we did at Easter
....

....

These are the visits and other special activities we did during my time at nursery
....

....

My favourite activity was
....

Here are the names of some special friends at nursery
....

....

....

Activities

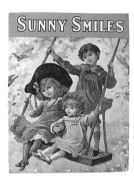

Parks

(Name of parks, first time on swing, favourite activities there, etc)

....

....

....

....

....

Library

(Name of library, first books borrowed, activities which

took place there)

....

....

....

....

Gym

(Gym clubs, or exercise activities, names of teachers)

....

....

....

....

Music

(Singing/music groups or lessons, teachers' names,

favourite songs/instruments)

....

....

....

Other activities

....

....

....

....

....

Travel

I first went on a long journey in a car on
....

We went to
....

and I saw
....

The first time I went on a train was
....

We went to
....

and I saw
....

I travelled on a bus for the first time on
....

We went to
....

and I saw
....

....

Photograph

The first time I travelled on an aeroplane was
....

The people who were with me were
....

....

....

....

We flew to
....

I went on a boat for the first time on
....

We went to
....

Entertainment

I went to the cinema for the first time when I was

....

The people who went with me were

....

The film we saw was

....

The first time we went to the theatre was on

....

The people who went with me were

....

The name of the show/play was

....

The first time I went to the circus was

....

My favourite act was

....

....

Other entertainments (puppet shows, magicians, etc)

Outings

Zoo

My first trip was on
....

to (name of zoo)
....

I went with
....

....

....

My favourite animals were
....

....

....

Photograph

Farm

My first trip was on
....

to (name of farm)
....

I went with
....

....

....

My favourite animals were
....

....

....

Photograph

Outings

Theme Park/Fun Fair

My first trip was on
....

to (name of place)
....

I went with
....

....

....

My favourite ride was
....

....

....

Museum

My first trip was on
....

to (name of museum)
....

I went with
....

....

....

What we saw
....

....

....

Photograph

Seaside

My first trip was on
....

to (name of place)
....

I went with
....

....

....

What we did
....

....

....

....

....

....

First Birthday

Birthday presents received

.... from
.... from
.... from
.... from
.... from
.... from

My favourite present was ....

I received .... birthday cards

Photograph

Friends invited to my party
....
....
....
....
....
....
....

Games we played
....
....
....
....

Second Birthday

Birthday presents received

	from
	from
	from
	from
	from
	from

My favourite present was

I received .... birthday cards

Photograph

Friends invited to my party

Games we played

Third
Birthday

Birthday presents received

.... from ....

.... from ....

.... from ....

.... from ....

.... from ....

.... from ....

My favourite present was ....

I received .... birthday cards

Photograph

Friends invited to my party

....

....

....

....

....

....

....

Games we played

....

....

....

....

Fourth
Birthday

Birthday presents received

	from
	from
	from
	from
	from
	from

My favourite present was

I received   birthday cards

Photograph

Friends invited to my party

Games we played

First Christmas

We spent Christmas Day at
....
with
....

Christmas presents received	
	from
	from
	from
	from
	from
My favourite present was	

My favourite present was
....

Photograph

What I had for my Christmas dinner:
....
....
....
....
....
....

(Memorable moments)
....
....
....
....
....
....

Second Christmas

We spent Christmas Day at
....
with
....

Christmas presents received	
....	from
....	from
....	from
....	from
....	from

My favourite present was
....

Photograph

What I had for my Christmas dinner:
....
....
....
....
....

(Memorable moments)
....
....
....
....
....
....

Third
Christmas

We spent Christmas Day at
....

with
....

Christmas presents received	
	from
	from
	from
	from
	from
My favourite present was	

Photograph

What I had for my Christmas dinner:
....
....
....
....
....

(Memorable moments)
....
....
....
....
....
....
....

Fourth
Christmas

e spent Christmas Day at
....

ith
....

Christmas presents received	
	from
	from
	from
	from
	from

My favourite present was
....

Photograph

What I had for my Christmas dinner:
....
....
....
....
....

(Memorable moments)
....
....
....
....
....
....
....

Our Happy Days

First Holiday

Where we went
....
on (date)

We stayed at
....

How we travelled
....

The people who went with us
....

What I liked best
....
....

The weather was
....
....

Photograph

Places visited/days out
....
....
....
....
....
....
....
....
....

Second Holiday

Where we went
....

on (date)
....

We stayed at
....
....

How we travelled
....
....

The people who went with us
....
....

What I liked best
....
....

Photograph

The weather was
....
....
....

Places visited/days out
....
....
....
....
....
....
....
....
....

Third Holiday

Where we went

....

on (date)

....

We stayed at

....

....

How we travelled

....

....

The people who went with us

....

....

What I liked best

....

....

The weather was

....

....

Places visited/days out

....

....

....

....

....

....

....

Photograph

Fourth Holiday

Where we went
....

on (date)
....

We stayed at
....

....

How we travelled
....

....

The people who went with us
....

....

What I liked best
....

....

The weather was
....

....

Photograph

Places visited/days out
....

....

....

....

....

....

....

....

....

....